ATTENTION:
A Special Note about how this book was created.

Dear Photographer,

Thank you for claiming your copy of "Behind the Lens: The Beginner's Guide to Finding and Unleashing Your Ability to See Creatively, So You Can Take Powerful Photographs... in 30 Days... With Any Camera."

This book will teach you critical mastering photography techniques, skills, tools, mindset and more that every photographer needs to understand and apply.

This book was originally created as a live interview.

That's why it <u>reads as a conversation</u> rather than a traditional "book" that talks "at" you.

I wanted you to feel as though I am talking "with" you, much like a close friend or relative.

I felt that creating the material this way would make it easier for you to grasp the topics and put them to use quickly, rather than wading through hundreds of pages.

So relax.

Grab a pen or pencil and some paper to take notes.

And get ready to take your mastering photography techniques to the next level so you can understand how to find and unleash your ability to see creatively so you can take powerful photographs with any camera.

Let's get started with taking beautiful photographs that impress with any camera right now…

Sincerely,
Herbert Innocent

YOUR JOURNEY BEGINS HERE

Herbert Innocent, Your #1 Mastering Photography Techniques Expert 3

Your First Step To Mastering Photography Techniques Success 15

The Next Step To Mastering Photography Technique Success 37

A Key Step For How To Find And Unleash Your Ability To See Creatively So You Can Take Powerful Photographs With Any Camera 57

The Next Steps For Beginner Photographers 69

Mastering Photography Techniques Tools Every Photographer Needs 73

The Perfect Mindset For Photographers 77

Mastering Photography Techniques Time Wasters 83

Mastering Photography Technique and Time Management 87

The Top Mastering Photography Techniques Challenges Beginner Photographers Face 95

Hidden Mastering Photography Techniques Opportunities 101

A Mastering Photography Techniques Case Study 107

Final Thoughts from Mastering Photography
Techniques Expert Herbert Innocent 115

Where To From Here.. 119

Serena: Hi, everyone, and welcome to **Behind The Lens: The Beginner's Guide to Finding and Unleashing Your Ability to See Creatively, So You Can Take Powerful Photographs… in 30 Days… With Any Camera**.

My name is Serena Cattacin.

Today I'm talking with mastering photography techniques expert, Herbert Innocent, about how every photographer can embark on the right track by mastering the best photography techniques to obtain the best result. Welcome, Herbert Innocent.

Herbert: Thank you. Thank you.

Serena: Herbert Innocent is a well-known expert on the subject of mastering photography techniques, and he has graciously consented to this interview to share with us the beginner's guide in this area so that every photographer can understand how to get started and how to find and unleash their ability to see creatively, so that you can take powerful photographs with any camera.

Herbert Innocent, thank you again for joining us on this live interview. Let's jump right in.

Herbert: Okay.

HERBERT INNOCENT, YOUR #1 MASTERING PHOTOGRAPHY TECHNIQUES EXPERT

Serena: My first type of question is about your background and experience in the field of mastering photography techniques so that photographers in our audience can understand who you are, where you're coming from and how you can relate to where they are right now.

So, we'll jump into the beginner steps to success that every photographer needs to understand in order to get going in the right direction. Could you tell us a little about yourself in terms of background, education and experience in mastering photography techniques?

Herbert: Okay. Yeah. So my background is as a self-taught photographer. I started taking my first photographs when I first got a small photography class. I took a small class in the summer when I was in high school. It ran for six hours in total in a single week, and it was just for fun.

And, from there, I really, really loved using the camera. And it wasn't very detailed, it just introduced us to a few rules when taking a photograph. And that was really the only education I ever had in taking photographs. Aside from that, everything else has been self-taught and I have been learning from experience. I've been building on from there to become a professional photographer ever since.

Serena: So, when did you get started?

Herbert: Well, I got started, if I remember correctly, probably in about 2012, and that's when I started walking around actively taking a few photos. But to really, really get into the craft and taking photos that I really was proud of, I started that in 2016, and that was after I had gone to Canada.

So, I had this opportunity. I was working and I wanted to help people. I had a chance to go and work with people with disabilities and I wanted to help empower them; I wanted to understand their environment and how I could use my skills to help them.

And so, I worked in a camp, a summer camp, up in the mountains in Canada, 2016, during... Sorry, yeah, in 2016 during the summer. And I had earned a little bit, a small amount of money, by the end of the camp. It wasn't enough to transfer it back to euros, though, and it was in Canadian dollars.

So, I decided I was going to buy something to take back. I was either going to buy a bicycle or a camera. I thought a bicycle would be too expensive to transport back so I bought a camera. And that was when my photography journey got started because now I had a basic professional camera to start using in my photography.

Serena: Such stuff, that was a nice beginning then. My next question is, have you had any formal training or education in mastering photography techniques, or have you been doing on-the-job training?

Herbert: So I would say it was mostly on-the-job training, I haven't had proper formal education. So the way I suppose it worked for me was, once I got the camera, I really wanted to be able to use it fully and master it. And I also wanted to share my artwork because through that summer camp, I think I discovered a new way for expressing myself that I didn't know.

The only way I could show what it felt to me was through art or some form of creative experience. And so, it was always on-the-job training, and it was very quick going from using the camera to getting hired and getting paid to use that camera. So, in that way, it was more of on-the-job training.

Serena: So, something very spontaneous and very direct from your soul. That's very nice and poetic to hear. What kinds of things have you done, or experiences, have you had in mastering photography techniques that are relevant to our audience of photographers, and our topic of taking beautiful photographs that impress with any camera.

Herbert: Okay. So, I've done all the way from sports photography. I've done a lot, and a lot of conference and event photography, and then I've done wedding photography. I've done animal photography, high-speed photography, night photography. I also did a lot of travel photography and portraits. I found that portraits and events were my favourite type of photography because it deals the most with humans, I felt like I was really connecting more with a lot more people.

I also did do a lot of landscape photography as well as, yeah, but for some reason it always came back to events, photographing events. These were corporate events, high profile events. I also did a lot of photography with, maybe you'd call them special occasions or private events, so this would be, like, a private meeting that would be very, very sensitive.

And it has to do with public relations... so when new contracts are being formed, when companies or different organizations, are signing up to new partnership contracts; usually they would like to have a photographer to show that this is a new beginning. I got a lot of experiences through that too you know... express that moment because it's a very unique one. It's not really an event, but it's also... it's a very special moment.

So I did a lot of photography in that, but overall, I think I've photographed just about everything I can think of. I mean, I used to travel a lot with my friend, we would go during the weekends or during the weekdays and we would challenge ourselves either to wake up at 4:00 AM, and then to go photographing around the town and we would photograph in Dublin all the way from 4:00 AM, let's say up to, I think it was 11:00 AM.

And we would photograph and then we'd do a lot of challenges like this, or we'd do a midnight challenge where we would photograph from sunset, all the way to 4:00 AM, just photographing, taking photographs. And we did a lot of these difficult photography challenges. And it was a lot of fun. I learned a lot from that because it was a lot of intensive hours, but we were relaxed. There wasn't any deadline.

It was to see how hard you can push your abilities and your camera to bring you that work you want. And so, as you can see, a lot of my experiences come from really going about in every single direction and then picking what specific areas I want to go to.

And, even though I personally would prefer photographing people, it's really people in any environment. For example, when I got started much, much earlier, I photographed a lot of street photography, and some of my best work has come from street photography. Even some of the work that a lot of my clients have really, really loved came from photographing people on the streets, just asking them, "hey, you look nice in your outfit. Can I take a photo of you?"

And I was surprised because most of them just say yes, yes. And, yeah. So, that's where a lot of my experience came from.

Serena: That's very, very inspiring, listening to your stories. If you can, or if you would like to pick one, which one is, like, let's say, the photo challenge that you liked the most, or that was more inspiring to you?

Herbert: I think the best photo challenge for me that I really, really loved was... we did a morning photography shoot where we started really early in the morning and we just walked around, and I found that to be one of my favourites because if the sun comes out, there's this time of the day where all the photos just looked so well because the lighting was perfect.

Although, it's really hard to pick one, but I thought that for me it was a perfect moment, because the energy in your body, is also just on the rise. As the sun is coming up, the level of energy in your body is also starting to rise up.

So, it's like you are waking up and the photography is getting better as the sun rises up into the day. So that was my favourite, I would say. Yeah.

Serena: Okay. So, rising together: your body, your soul and your photos as well. Okay. Where do you feel an overnight success or did you have to work for it?

Herbert: So I think I wouldn't even call it an overnight success, I would call it a work in progress from my point of view. And the reason why I would call that is because I feel like you can always improve it and it's always developing. It's always developing and there's so many art styles and I think I had to work really hard to get to where I got, but it didn't feel like I was working hard because I felt like I was also lucky enough to find the right steps.

Because it can take quite a long time, there's a lot that cameras can do these days, and you can get stuck on getting the right lens, or finding that perfect filter, or flash, or you can get really easily distracted with getting the equipment and knowing the equipment and you can forget that this is just an art form that requires being mastered.

And so, I think I worked really hard to get there. I also think that I was lucky enough to be able to work in a way that allowed me to get there faster.

It would have taken much, much longer because I know there are courses out there that you may have to take for the entire year before you can really be able to take work that you're proud of.

Serena: Okay, sure. The keywords or the expression, the main expression is work in progress, I would say. How did you come up with an idea of this book, or what makes you want to write this book?

Herbert: So I think one of the things that I've also learned is, when I was teaching myself photography, I noticed that a lot of photography talked about the camera. They say use this flash for this, use this setting to do this part. For example, if you're taking a portrait, they'll focus on using a portrait lens and things like that. But one thing I really never heard was the mindset. So, for example, every time you're doing something, I think you need to have the right mindset, and I never got the right mindset. So, even though they'll tell me all these rules, for example, one of the rules is there's the golden hours.

So, in the morning and in the evening when the sun is just low enough, the clouds look great and the sun is not very strong on the subject. Those are called golden hours because when you take photos on those, the lighting on the subject is usually really, really good.

And they'll tell you all the rules and all these processes that you can follow, but they never quite talk about mindset.

So, I've looked at a lot of tutorial books and they don't really talk about the mindset that you need to have. And I think that it's important that, if you're going to go and create a piece of work, your work, especially if it's an art, I think it needs to have a message because you are creating something that people are going to engage in, and you want people to be able to engage with your work the way you want them to engage so that it can have an impact on them in their life.

Whether you want them to make an active decision, whether you want them to think of something differently, whether you want them to realize something that they never realized before, that is a message that you want to come from your work.

And so, most photography courses, photography books, talk about how to use your camera. And they're usually manual. They're giving you all these settings, but they don't tell you how to think as a photographer. And not necessarily tell you, but even guide you, as in, if you want to take these kinds of photos and you want to create this message, they don't guide you on how to create this message.

And so, as a photographer, you are stuck with the process of, "I have to take a thousand photos so I know how to take a photo that creates this message."

And I thought, that's a very long process of learning. I think there could be a shortcut and I thought this could be one way of creating a shortcut that helps you create the right mindset so that you can go and create a message with your photography work. So that every photo you take has the right message that you want it to say, rather than taking a photo and then hoping it's going to have the right message.

Serena: So, we will go in depth today about the photographer's mindset.

Herbert: Yes.

Serena: Well, it's obvious you're the right expert for us when it comes to mastering photography techniques. Let's get started with the beginner's guide.

Herbert: Okay.

YOUR FIRST STEP TO MASTERING PHOTOGRAPHY TECHNIQUES SUCCESS

Serena: What is the FIRST step beginner photographers need to take with mastering photography techniques and taking beautiful photographs that impress with any camera?

Herbert: So, from my point of view, I think the first thing that every photographer should do to get started is ask themselves: why are they taking a photo?

So, in the previous question I touched a little bit about the idea of having a message, and I think it is crucial that as a photographer, you ask yourself why. The reason why you want to ask yourself that question is because just thinking about it helps you frame your photograph very, very differently, and by framing I mean the position from which you are taking the photograph.

If you know why you want to take the photograph, you might even decide, "okay, I need to change the angle that I am taking this photograph." And, just like that, you've added another creative element to your work just by thinking about why am I taking this photograph?

And there could be many reasons why you're taking that photograph, but there's a very big difference between taking a photo on purpose versus just taking a photo because it looks pretty. I mean, anyone can press that shutter button to take a photo on the camera, even a five year old can do that, but the difference between really good photography work and any photo, I think, is the intention. Some photographers go as far as creating the stage, setting up the scenery as you need it to be.

So, for example, they may have to clean the environment to remove the things they don't want, just so they can take that photo. And it looks really good in the end because they did the preparation, there were intentions, they saw a vision of the photo, they asked why, they asked what will look really good in this scenario, what to do...

And, by asking why, it also means you can decide "what can I not keep in the environment" because the camera will just capture everything coming in. And so, I think, and I've come to learn this the hard way: that asking why really helps you create a very good quality photograph. So, yeah.

Serena: Okay. So, why is the question. But my question is, why is it important that this is the first step?

Herbert: Well, so, for starters, if you are taking photographs...

So let's take a few scenarios here. So, if you take the first scenario where you are taking a photograph for, let's say, a client, by asking yourself why am I taking this photograph, in my case, if you use my example, if I pick one of my clients as an event photographer, I was taking photography for events that were designed to empower people, so these were conference events or start-up events.

And, when I was taking those photographs, I asked myself why. You should ask yourself, why are you taking these photographs? And that means you will try to understand what your client is trying to do, why they would need that photo. And, in this case, my client wanted to show how empowering and impactful their events were.

And so, in order for me to understand that, I needed to understand who my client was. I needed to understand what they wanted to do, and I needed to understand what I can do to help them do what they're trying to do better.

And to do that, there's a few tricks that I did to get there, but I suppose to do all that means that not only do you know what you are doing but you know the reasons why you are doing it. So, I suppose the importance of this is if you want to take photographs that your clients are happy to see, then you need to understand why you are taking that photograph. In the same way that if you want to take a photograph that has a message to communicate that message in the magazine, in a newspaper or in a gallery, it's the same process.

As a photographer, you need to know why you are taking that photo, why from that angle, why in that way, why with the lens you use, because each element contributes differently.

As a quick example, if you use a wide angle lens versus a portrait lens to take a photograph of a person, they come out very, very different. They're the same person, everything is the same, but the way they look is a little bit different. And so you can use that to your creative advantage.

Because you know why you are taking that photo, you may want to create a certain feeling; by just changing the lens, you can create that feeling. And another example is by asking why, you also begin to see how many ways you could try and take the same photograph to get to a photo that really says what you want it to say. So, that'll be the one reason why you would want to do that.

Serena: So, the photographer might be focused on the message and the purpose of the photo itself?

Herbert: Yes.

Serena: So, my next question is, what's the best way for them to take this first and essential step?

Herbert: Okay. So, I think the best way to do that is to really understand your subject and the best way to do that is to pick one way, rather than to try and do them all. It's okay to try them all and then pick one way, but to try and do it all will limit how much growth you can get in one area.

For example, there's landscape photography and there's portraits, and there are events, and there's animal photography, and there's all these other types of photography. What I have found is events and portraits tend to go together because they deal a lot with people. And then, I also found landscape and real estate photography also go together.

So, by picking one type of photography, you really focus on how to create a really good mood with each type because I think photography is ultimately about creating a feeling, an expression, and the best way to do that is to understand by picking one and then understanding how to create the mood in those ones.

Because how you create a mood in landscape photography is slightly different to how you create a mood in portrait photography. And so the best way to take a step is first, by deciding, "okay, I want to focus on this area."

And, if you pick portrait photography, then that means you're going to be focusing on understanding why you are taking a photograph of this person. And, let's say, if this is a client and you want to take a photo, an artistic photo of them, one of the few things that a lot of photographers will do is ask the client to tell them a little bit about themselves, so, getting to know the client, and then after you've gotten to know the client, then you may decide to create the environment in which the clients feel more themselves.

Because, most of the time, the client will actually be nervous about being in front of the camera. And so, by creating that environment where they can be themselves, then you make it easier for them to allow you to take photos that shows them who they really are in the course.

So, that's just one of the ways to do it. There are other ways, but it really comes down to understanding your environment, understanding your subject, and then also understanding your message that you want to create and then manipulating the environment so that you can show your message coming through your subject in your photograph.

Serena: So, when I was listening to your three terms, let's say, it's me, like, it's my interest in the words' subject, environment and the message. I think that they are like three, let's say, keywords. Can you go into a little more detail on this? Maybe giving us more details about one of your pictures or clients.

Herbert: Okay. So, if I go into an example of…

So, I'm going to stick with events for a little while just because everyone can relate to events. So, one case that I remember was I talked about environment, subject, and being able to manipulate those, and if I should use the case of my clients, my event client as an example, what I would say is... so, let's say I wanted to create a photograph that really expressed what the event looked like and in most cases, most of my clients were managers or event managers, and what I needed to do was understand what my client wanted to show in their photos, and what they wanted to show was excitement, empowerment, and they wanted to show impactful. They want to show those three things in their photograph.

There was more they could say, but those were the biggest things because, at the end of the day, I knew that my clients would use these photos either on big banners, and they did use some of them on the big banners. They wanted to use them on magazines, they wanted to use them on newsletters, they wanted to use them on their website, they wanted to use them in their booklets and books. And I knew because a lot of my photos had been used in this way before, including in the newspapers. So, they wanted as soon as someone sees this photograph, the person will stop and look at the photo. And so, they wanted this photo to show how the event was engaging, empowering as well as impactful.

So, whenever I was taking a photo, I needed to go and decide, "okay, so my client is trying to achieve these results. These are their goals. How can I make this event show that moment?"

And so, one of the best things that I did to try and show those moments was to realize that first of all, I'm going to have to take charge of specific elements of the event. And, with one case, some of my clients allowed me to re-arrange where the subjects were vastly, so, telling the participants of the events where they would sit.

So we would put, let's say, a lot of people in the front row, so that when you're taking photos from the front of the event venue, you'd see very well where the subjects are. They'll be very well lit, they'll be close to the camera, and then you'll see them very well.

Then the other thing we'll do, as an example, will be when the participants of the events, in this case those I've called the subjects, when they are talking to each other, when in that candid conversation like the way you and me are talking, so when they are talking to each other, I wanted to show how energetic and engaged they were. So, I would look for those key moments.

And then, another thing I would look for is when they are in the heat of the moment. So, for example, something happened and they're very happy; you'll see them clapping, you'll see them talking, you see that wave of joy coming out of them. And so, as the photographer, you'll be like a hunter trying to get those moments to take those photographs.

Because just by waiting, timing and capturing those few key moments, you instantly and I mean very, very quickly create the emotions that you really want. And even though sometimes the events may be either small or big, all these things become irrelevant because, as a photographer, you took complete control of the stage and you brought that out to life.

Another really good example where the client was really surprised and happy was when I was doing a small shooting for a Taekwondo club. And, in this case, my client essentially was teaching young kids how to do Taekwondo. Now, I'm going to mix between karate and Taekwondo because I'm not so sure what the difference is.

But I remember it was these little kids between the ages of 4 to 12, if I remember correctly, and they were practicing these moves, and if you're looking at them in real world, I suppose from her point of view, when she was looking at them, it was just kids moving. They didn't look like they could put a serious punch.

But when I was taking photographs, I was looking

for those moments when the child is really striking because to me, the subject, depending on how you look at them, to me, that's when they were having their best moment.

So, in my point of view, they were really good at what they were doing, because I was looking for those moments and taking those photographs to show them at their best, because they're practicing to be their best. They're practicing their aim to be better and to show those proud moments to show that they've done what they're trying to do. Whether it's a kick and the leg is right up in the air, and it's a four year old but the leg is really up high in the air, and that they're grabbing each other.

And so, I'll take these moments, and by just selectively timing to take those moments, I was able to show them doing really, really quality work... as in, capable of doing what the master, who is my client teaching them, wants them to do. And she was surprised how I was able to show them. And it wasn't even a work of Photoshop or anything; it was just timing and taking the right photo at the right time. With the right mindset, you're able to create the message that is really, really desired. Yeah. So, that's that.

Serena: So, we can say that you catch the spontaneous and real moments.

Herbert: Yes, yes.

Serena: If I would like instruments, like, I'm going to ask you if there are any tools, websites, or apps that make this first step easier for our photographers?

Herbert: So, from my point of view, I think there are tools that can help you. But I think one of the best tools that I got was... I remember this one time where I... Actually, earlier on, I decided I really wanted to understand who my clients were because I wanted to help them achieve their goal. Now, my point of view is one where I'm focusing on the client, but I also do equally focus on the subject.

So the way I focused on the client, the tool I used was... It was this: I took a paper and I decided to create... There's this concept in marketing called creating an avatar, a customer avatar, and what that means essentially is you take a piece of paper and then you write down what you know about your client in terms of what are their goals, so, what are they trying to achieve with their goals, what are their desires, so what outcome do they desire that they want to achieve? What is their roadblock, so, what things are stopping them from getting those outcomes? And what are their fears, things that are preventing them from taking actions to get to where they want?

And, by writing these down, I had a lot more

questions than that, and it's some of the questions that I had included. So, what they're doing, maybe where they live, what kind of busy lifestyle they had, and by understanding all these things, I was able to put down enough information on a piece of paper to try and get an understanding of who my clients were, who all my subjects were.

And so I did that, and in most cases, some of the information was very limited. So if I knew my client, what job they were doing, I would look for a typical job post... so, let's say for example, if it's an event manager, I will look for an event manager job post, and I would see the requirements and then-

I could see what my client's goals were, right? And then I could see what kind of things will be preventing them from looking like the best event manager possible. And I'll try and see what I can do with my photography to really compensate for those things when I'm photographing the work for them, because this was who I was focusing myself to help serve.

So, the tool I use will be that kind of paper where you'd put a customer avatar and there are lots and lots of different types of examples online, but for me, that was the biggest one that really put a shift in terms of how I understand who my clients were, or who my subjects were. And, even though I'm referring to them as my clients, in most cases they were both my clients and my subjects, as in, when I was taking photographs of them.

And another way to also get even more detail into this is, as an example, when I'm taking photographs of let's say a portrait. What I would do is, sometimes the portrait will be very limited short of time. I've had a lot of cases where I'll be hired to take photographs of 20 people back to back within an hour or so, or maybe a little bit more like two hours or something like that.

And that will mean that I would have about five minutes per person. Five or less minutes and in those five minutes, I am supposed to prepare the person, take a photo of the person, make sure they are happy with the photo and then move on. And, in this case, there is no time to go and start researching every person's job and what they like, what they had for breakfast...

So, what I'll do is, just when you're taking photograph, I will ask them, do they have a favourite angle that they like to take photos from? Most of them wouldn't know, but these small conversations would help. I would also give them a few tips, like, before you come to the photograph the next day I would say,

"just make sure when you're coming in, make sure

you're holding a warm cup of coffee or something, a cup of tea, because it will boost up your confidence."

So, I will use all these small psychological tricks to have them feel prepared. I'll tell them,

"iron your clothes so that when you're taking a photo it shows you in your best professional light possible."

I'll give them all these small tips in an email or circulating it to them to make sure that they're all prepared and they have everything so that, when I'm taking the photos, they are all ready and then, during the set, one of the few things I'd asked them to do to create that environment is I'll tell them, "just don't worry about the camera, just go to your favourite place in your mind and then look at the top of the camera over here,

and then don't worry about me, I'll just take a photo whenever they are ready and I may take a few photos… "

And, with each photo, I'll double check with them just so they are feeling confident, that they're happy with the photo and if you don't like something, we talk. We say,

"okay, so you don't like this part, we will try the same photo, we will just change this small thing here."

And so, we will keep going like that, but by working like that it means I am working with them to create the message that they want to say about themselves. Because, at the end of the day, it doesn't matter what photo you're taking of. You're trying to say something. You want to say, I'm a professional and this is me, and the photo can speak volume.

So, getting it right the first time round, especially in a world where someone can look you at your LinkedIn profile and be like, "oh, okay,"

So, you want your photograph to speak, to say the right message, because these are the things that you're using to build relationships. So, the best tool for me was that customer avatar, and then understanding a little bit of the psychology to help my customer not feel afraid of the camera because a lot of people are not very comfortable with cameras.

So, finding ways to help them overcome that nervousness that we feel when there's a camera looking right in our face.

Serena: I will confess I am one of those ones who don't feel comfortable at all in front of a camera. So listening that there is someone who is trying to have this kind of gentle approach to the person who would be the subject of the photo is very reassuring.

So, we consider the first step is more or less about trying to get to know more or understand better the client. So, it's about collecting information... creating an identity, I would say, during a first picture of him or her, doing this, like, through let's say more gentle but very significant gestures.

Herbert: Yes.

Serena: I understand very, very well. And, like, you have already mentioned these, but I would like to ask you maybe one example, let's say the most positive that you had or the most bizarre about how long does it take this first step? to get to know a client, do you have a specific one with whom you had very simple direct connection, or another opposite case when you struggled to get to know him or her?

Herbert: Okay. So, in my case, sometimes it just takes five minutes to get to know the person and to take the photo of them that they are happy with. And the longer you do it, I think it comes with practice a little bit and building up a list of things that you can do with a person to help them overcome that fear.

I had a case of this client and she was not very... she would never smile in front of the camera and to me. I knew I could make her feel good and take a photo that she would be happy about but she wouldn't smile. And then I asked her... I took a few photos and then we talked a little bit and then I asked her, "well, how do you feel about cameras?"

And then she said, "I don't like them because I've never liked a photo of them."

And then I told her, "Well, I can make this process enjoyable."

And then, just by saying that and just being reassuring, that will show you what I'm doing exactly. If you're not happy, we'll delete everything. She was comfortable and she was happy to try because at the end of the day, the fear is in our mind and we want to help them overcome it, right?

I mentioned the roadblocks, right? They desire to show themselves in the best way, but there's this roadblock, there's this fear, or there is this thinking or mindset that they have on their head and it's not their fault. No one's fault. It just happens. You've seen something you don't like before in the past or whatever the reason may be and so, as the photographer, it's your job to say, "I can help you overcome that," and to say that in the right way so that you are not making anyone feel alienated.

And so, for me, I would say most cases in five minutes or less I've learned to be able to turn around, to take a complete stranger who we've never talked to before and just be able to create a very nice photo of them, where they are smiling, confident and feeling that they are the best themselves there. And some of the best ways I do that is by telling them, "think of your favourite place."

And other ways that I would do that is by showing them the photograph and saying, " do you like this angle or do you want to try something else different?" By giving them that option they also feel like, oh, I'm also doing this with you. So let's try something else. Let's see what happens. And sometimes, they go a little bit crazy, which is really, really good because then it allows you to bring out an even more expressive side of themselves.

And what you want to hear at the end is when their friends say, "that is so much like them." And that usually are the other expressions that you'd hear later on, they say that is so much like him or that is so much like her, and that at the end, there it's all about the experience. Yeah.

The photograph will be one moment. It will be one sec, one millisecond or one microsecond, or however long it will take to produce it. But it's also the experience that you give to the client. And that experience ultimately is also kept within the photograph. So, it's not just a photo that other people are going to see, but it's also how the client

	sees it and how they feel when they see it. So, I think there's a lot more to it than just one step and you're gone. So, I hope that answered the question.
Serena:	Yes. Yes, it did. It's about a process more than just one singular step. And let's say the best achievement is to get a photo which is authentic. If I understood correctly, that's very, very important. But if someone gets stuck on this step, say if one of our photographers were stuck… What kind of advice you would like to give them, how can they get unstuck?
Herbert:	Okay. So I think the best way to get unstuck on this is, well, so there are many ways you can take a photograph, but the best thing to do is if you're stuck is maybe go back to the basics, right? And the basics is, if you're going to take a photograph, just know why… Just ask yourself, what do I want to say? The best way to find that out so that you're never stuck is to ask yourself, what do you like, what do you want?
	If you could have a message say something about you, what would it be? Because I heard a mentor of mine said… he was running all this business and one morning he just woke up and really hated his business. And I feel like I've been there a little bit.
	He hated it because he was working but even though it was good business, he wasn't seeing

much progress. And he felt like, is this what it is going to be like, this is what it is going to always be like, and he wanted to understand what kind of people he wanted to serve. And I think that's really, really important.

So even if you may not be shooting as a professional photographer, you may be doing this just for fun, maybe for your family, but what message do you want to say about your family? Are they fun people? Are they always happy? Do they have a serious and funny side to them? Are they all the same? Do they have individual personalities?

So, there's that way to look at it, and another way to look at it would be to ask yourself, what do you want your work to say about you? And that may not be too much in helping you get unstuck, but that is the best way to start. You can start by saying, well, I love wild photography. What do I want to say about animals?

Anyone can take a photo of a bird, but what do you want to say about animals? What do you want to say about birds? What do you want your photograph to communicate?

And, by focusing on that, then your mind will try to constantly show you different angles, different ways to use your camera, to say what you want to say, as opposed to trying and figuring out all the different ways we could use your cameras by focusing on asking why you will naturally try to see and find places and opportunities where you can take the same photo, but with something different each and every time. And that makes the whole difference in helping you get unstuck. If that makes sense.

Serena: Okay. So we can say that, when someone is stuck… re-questioning your motivation might be, let's say, the solution.

Herbert: Yes. Yes.

Serena: So what we have been talking about was just the first step of a long and articulate process. So, if you agree, now we can move to the second step.

Herbert: Yes.

THE NEXT STEP TO MASTERING PHOTOGRAPHY TECHNIQUE SUCCESS

Serena: And my question is, what is the SECOND step beginner photographers need to take with mastering photographic techniques and taking beautiful photographs that impress with any camera?

Herbert: Okay. So I think the second step will be to master your camera, to know your camera. And I don't mean to know every single thing it can do. I still don't know. And I know a lot of photographers just focus on one thing and that you could also know them over time, everything that it can do. But I think one of the best ways is to know your cameras so that each time you pick it up, you know just what to do to create the effect you want.

And this could mean understanding how the different modes work. And I won't go into any complicated technicals. There's a lot of books that go into the different technical of how the cameras work. But, as an example, I would say knowing how to shoot in a manual mode is a one good way of being able to get started.

And there's a lot of tips. But one thing I would say is just knowing about five, six or seven settings, not too many, five, six or seven settings. So, knowing a setting for portraits, a standard setting for portraits, and then finding a standard setting for landscapes. And, when I say standard, these aren't already made standard… it isn't defined by industry or anything. I just mean standard to you.

So, for example, if you've ever taken a very good portrait, find the best manual settings to defined your standard, the idea is by finding a few key things that you understand, then you can start to expand your comfort zones from there, right? Because the whole experience will be like exploring on the map.

You want to know what you know, the places you know on the map, so that when you go out, you don't get lost. You can go out and come back to the places where you know and then keep exploring from there. You want to treat your camera like that because it can get very complicated, very quickly, and as a way to start very quickly, one of the things I would say would be grab your camera and then choose a focus point and then choose...

So if you're taking photographs of portraits, or if you are taking a landscape, then choose a setting for one of those and then try and master taking photographs with those settings. Because the difference really is because there's the rules that you can use to make photographs look good and there's camera settings, and a lot of photographers get lost there.

I know because I was there and it takes a very long time to overcome and I'll try and shortcut that process, but it comes down to picking one thing and understanding it before you try to move on. If I'm saying that correctly, does that make sense?

Serena: So, the second step is basically about picking a specific setting and working on it.

Herbert: Yes, yes. Basically mastering photography. Sorry, mastering your camera.

Serena: Okay. And how do they do it? I mean, what kind of advice can you give going more in depth or in detail?

Herbert: Okay. So the first way to do it would be... So, the way I learned to do this was I realized that... what I learned was if you're going to take a photograph that tells a message, you need to understand that you are controlling where the person is looking. So, when a person looks at a photograph, humans won't look at the entire photograph at once.

They will look at a point on a photo and then try to move their eyes around the photograph to see the entire photo. That also happens to be how we look in real life. So, when you're looking at things in your real life, we first look at one thing, whatever it is that grabs our attention first, and then try to look at the rest of everything afterwards. Now, where most people get confused is when they take a photograph their settings will either be in auto or semi-automatic.

And so what that means is that there'll be a lot of information captured in the photograph. And, when you're looking at the photograph, a lot of things are jumping out of the person. And so, the photograph doesn't convey an impactful message anymore because, to convey an impactful message, you want to control where the person is looking at as soon as they try to glance at that photo.

And, in most cases, I'll use the portrait as an example. If you're taking photos of a person or an animal, you want to make sure that the eyes are the focus point... so when we are looking at a photo of a portrait, we usually look at the eyes first. So, whether it's an eye of an animal or a human or a person, we look at the eyes, and then we look to the rest of the photo.

So, if you know, this is the logic that we use to look, then you need to try and use that to your advantage. You can then be creative. Do you want to make sure that the eyes are blurred out, or do you want to make sure that the eyes are very sharp and in focus and clear to see, because depending on what you do, you can then have a creative element. And that speaks a different message.

For example, if the eyes can't be seen, the person's looking down, then you can think maybe he or she is shy. Or, if in the photos they are looking up, I think usually it's to the right or to the left, they can either be looking very hopeful or maybe trying to look at something that caught their attention. And so, you can already see they are creating different messages by just knowing where the person is looking, where their eyes are looking, I haven't even gone to talk about anything else just by focusing on creating very specific, understanding, small details.

In this section, here what I'm talking about is understanding your camera and what the camera does for you in this case. Let's say you're taking a photo of a portrait of a person... What you want to do is you want to make sure you know how to focus, right? So, if you're taking a portrait of a person, the eyes are the key things of interest. You want to be able to focus on the eyes, and if the eyes aren't the key thing of interest, then you want to focus on whatever it is that is the key thing of interest.

And then, knowing your camera means you can also control how much detail your camera has. One example is to know your focus; there is ultra focus and the other different versions of focus.

So, the one that I use is single point focus and this is the focus that I feel like it's a manual focus. It just means that I select a point that my camera will focus on. And I find that very, very useful in cases of portraits. If you're doing landscape, then you could use this for landscape as well or you could use a multi focus, where you have multiple points to focus on for landscape and that works really well.

So, with focus we can control the level of detail. The other thing I want to talk about is how much information you show in a photograph. And the amount of information that is shown in the photograph can be in two ways. One is by deciding what is within the frame of your photograph and the other would be by deciding what is being seen clearly versus what is not very clear, what is blurry in the background.

And you do that by being able to control your lens. By being able to select and control your lens. That's why there's all these different types of lens. So if you take in this case, if you're using a portrait lens or if you're using a Zoom lens, what you want to do is you want to use a setting that will allow you to essentially make sure that you have just the right amount of information in focus.

Again, I won't go into too much detail on settings because there's a lot of books talking about a lot of settings, and I don't want you to get lost in settings. I want you to have this mindset so that when you pick a camera, you are thinking because it's easy to see the setting and then copy it, but it's very hard to create the photo without the mindset.

And the mindset is, if you want to create a photograph with a message, then you have to understand: what do you not want that message to say? And how can you remove that additional information. And the way you do it is by knowing your camera, for example, the best way to remove information will be either to frame it differently, so to take a photograph from a different angle, or to make that information out of focus, or to shoot the photograph through something. And in that way, you're creating a natural frame for which the person will think with your framing... You're giving them a way to think.

So, this is a lot of different things, and it's going to be a lot just to cover even knowing your camera could be an entire book on its own, but for this purpose, I'm hoping that I made sense by saying that by knowing your camera, I don't mean remembering all the settings. I just mean understand what you can use to create a different mood.

And sometimes you can shoot in automatic and still create very different moods. I'm not saying you can't, you can definitely do that. Understand what mode, what kind of mood and message you want to say and understand how your camera can do that for you.

Serena: So, I was listening very carefully to your answer and I was thinking, we can say if the first step is about getting to know your clients or the subject of your picture, then the second is about getting to know your camera.

Herbert: Yes.

Serena: So, understanding the camera, understanding how you can use it, according to your purpose, like what you want to shoot with your camera, is that right?

Herbert: Yes.

Serena: And even for the second step, let's see, are there any tools, websites or apps that make these steps easier?

Herbert: I think there are a lot of tutorials on how to take... or maybe how to set your camera differently. So, I mentioned that there is a lot of tutorial on how to set your camera, so you can take a photograph with different environmental settings, how you control different settings for different atmospheres.

And just as a small hint, I usually just control about four things on my camera and that's all I've ever done because there's quite a lot of settings, but I've decided to only control four things. And that is all I ever do. And in most cases, I even narrow down that to about three things. So, there are the big words that they use like exposure, shutter speed and what do you call that? Maybe the focus points.

Though I usually control more the focus point and the shutter speed. Those are usually the key. So, for my portraits, whenever I'm trying to take a photo of a portrait, what I've learned is the lower you lower your focus points, sorry, the lower you lower your... essentially, by making sure that your lens are open as wide as possible, you can capture as much natural of a person as possible. So, I'm trying not to go into the technical details, here, because if I am honest, I've avoided knowing or understanding those myself.

It can get quite confusing and very technical, but what I mean is, usually there's three things that you want to understand about your camera and that is, you want to understand what your camera can do in different environments, because there are limits to what your camera can do and sometimes this can be frustrating. And let me explain to you what I mean by that.

So, in most cases, when someone takes a photo, they're immediately thinking that the photo represents reality, what you see in the real world, but in most cases that is not true and the reason being because there's only so much information that the photograph can capture. And so you have to give it the best settings to present what you see in real life. But what you forget is when you're looking in real life, you don't see the same as when you're looking at a photograph, because in real life things are open to interpretation, right?

We could be looking at the same thing, but we are thinking about different things. But when you take a photograph, you are trying to force everyone to see the same thing and think the same thing at the same time.

And so, that can be a little bit different. So when it comes to, how can you learn more about this step, like tools, websites, and things like that, I would say you can use YouTube as one of the key points on how to take these steps in understanding your camera, because those will be best cases where you will see a person using a specific setting to achieve a specific effect.

But before you can do that, you need to know what effect you want to achieve. Otherwise, you'll be trapped in the loop of knowing 1000 different effects but not sure how to use even one of them, because you will forget if you try to learn many things, and the goal here is to try and remember less, right?

You want to do less work for yourself. You want to do yourself a favour by knowing what you need so you can only take what you need and forget about the rest because it's unnecessary or it'll only overload and make it harder for you. So YouTube would be... I'll say, at the beginning, I learned a lot by looking at what I wanted to achieve and looking at who had done that and how they did it and borrowing a few of the things.

Now, one thing to be cautious of is you can get into the trap of needing to buy what the other person has, who is using this. And this can be quite a huge problem where you see most photographers get trapped into the idea of buying more equipment, buying more lenses, buying flashlights, buying studio lights, just to capture a portrait, but you don't need all this, right?

And that's why I'm a little bit hesitant to try... I'm trying to be careful not to mislead you here because a lot, I mean, every beginner photographer will get trapped at least once in this loop where they are thinking, if only I could have this lens, I'll be able to do this.

You know, you don't need all that and that's why, I mean, know your camera as opposed to getting another camera or getting another lens. So what I mean is, understand what your camera can do with what you have, because you can almost definitely achieve similar effects with everything that your camera has. So, some of my earliest photographs were in or on the phone, even after I had gotten the camera, I use the phone. It was a HTC, and I was still able to achieve if not very very similar effects with the photograph that I took on the phone, as I could with my camera.

And so, in this here, the goal is to understand the camera and the best way to do that is to know what you want to do. And then search for someone who is doing that with the settings and the equipment that you have. And if you don't have studio lights and all these things, you don't need to get them to achieve the same effect. You can use natural lighting, or you can use other forms of lighting, like just the normal lighting in the house and you can achieve a lot of effects. It all comes down to understanding the camera instead of buying more equipment.

Serena: Okay. So, thinking about time, how long does this step take, like, if you want to compare with the changes, if you have changed it from the beginning of your career to, like, nowadays?

Herbert: Okay. I think this step is actually quite a continuous process and I think it does take long because every time you take a new photo, you learn something new. And sometimes it takes a while before you can understand something because you don't know what you're doing wrong. One thing that really helped me overcome this was I used to record down the settings that I was using.

So, when I take a photograph, I would have a

document in a folder with those photographs with the settings that I used. So, I have documents for my portraits and have documents from my event photography.

And then, whenever I would go back to an event, I would record, I would use those settings, or just set them up on the camera the night before when I'm charging the batteries and preparing everything. And then I would use those the next day and the only thing that I would have to change would be if the different lighting, the different focus points and when I'm zooming in and out, and those are just very very small things to do.

So, there's a way you can definitely set in if this is something that would be of interest. I may create additional material here just to really shortcut the entire process, because it really is about having a specific setting. But the problem with this is everyone is going to be doing something different and what you want to do is you want to find the basic standard setting.

You want to know that, and that can take just a few minutes. It's a few minutes of Googling it, knowing what your camera is and knowing what it can do. But this is also going to be subject to a different opinions…

Because if you want to take a photograph with the basic camera and with a basic lens, what you want to do is you want to find the best settings for that scenario. And, because there's so many different lenses, so many different versions of camera, that means there are exponentially that many different types of settings. So, the best way to do that is to essentially just take your camera, take a photograph and record the settings that you like the photograph came out of.

And then, next time, try to explore around that or find the photograph that someone already took with the camera that we are using and the lens that we're using and that you really love, and then record that. And that's really just a few minutes. Flickr's a very good place where photographers have recorded their photos and the lens that they used, so you can see that very, very quickly. And, if you like it, you can then decide, okay, so, to create this effect, I just need to use these settings here.

Serena: That's very interesting advice. And in case someone anyway will get stuck, do you have any other suggestions about it?

Herbert: Yeah. So, I think this is a process where people are going to get stuck. And I know the only way to get unstuck on this process is going to be to just trust yourself and remind yourself that this is a learning process. The first few photos are going to frustrate you, and they're going to frustrate you for a very simple reason.

Either you're going to find the photo you like that you can't achieve the settings you want because you're missing something. Either you're missing a flash, either you're missing a lens or either you're missing the model type of the camera, so you have a different camera. And so, you feel like you can't achieve the different settings.

And I'll give you a personal example here. A personal example of mine was, I saw this photograph I really liked. It was a portrait. And I realized that one of the settings on the shutter speed and the shutter speed is how fast the shutters in the camera are going to close.

How fast they will open and then close to stop the light from keep going in the camera. And so, I remember when I first got started, I saw a photograph I really liked but the setting that camera had was not possible on my camera because I was using the basic model. And what I realized was that, I couldn't achieve that mood I wanted to create in the same way, I had come and create it around.

So, I had to find my way around that. And one thing I've learned is those limitations aren't a problem, they are actually an opportunity for you to discover because with every limitation, it means you can create something that wasn't possible by looking through those limits and finding your way around it.

So, what I did to create a photo that came close to what I wanted there was to understand essentially what my settings were and to understand how close I could come to that. And if I couldn't get that, that means I could achieve by manipulating the environment. So, there are three things that you can control when coming to take a camera. You can control the environment; you can control the camera setting and you can control the... how do you call that?

The post-production of the photograph. So, once you've taken the photograph, after you've taken it, you can also control a few things in there. So, if you can't control the camera, then you just have to control the environment and then control what the photo looks like in the end. With a little bit of editing and final retouching, you can get it to look very, very similar to what you want.

And, in most cases, there is more than one way to say the same message, and the best way to know how to say the same message is to know the psychology of how the person thinks. And you don't even need to know too much. You will learn this as soon as you discover why you want to take the photograph because you realize even in movies, they use similar tricks.

When the person is feeling hopeful, what do they look like in the movies? If you see that in the movies, you can create the same effect with the photograph. And as soon as you realize what you want to achieve, you'll start seeing a lot of examples in the different place.

So, the best way to get unstuck on this process is basically to simply go back again to the basics... What message do you want to say, and how can you go different about it? Because otherwise it's a game of seeing who can buy all the camera equipment. Very, very quickly, you begin to feel like you need to buy every single thing in the camera shop just to take the same photo, and you don't want to do that because it's really expensive, right?

Serena: Good. So, to sum up this second section, we can say that it is about getting to know your camera and usually we need just to manage three or four elements about it. And it's mostly a learning process, continuous learning process, where problems are not limits; most of the time, they are new opportunities.

Herbert: Yes. And just add on that, one thing I would say is when I say know your camera, maybe I should say, know what your camera can do to help you say the message you want to say. Maybe that's the best way to put it. So, know what your camera can do to help you create the message you want to create. So, instead of knowing everything that your

	camera can do, just know what your camera can do to help you create your message.
Serena:	Good. Okay. So, that's very interesting and important. And back to basics, we can say it's the most important expression here to use.
Herbert:	Yes. Yes.

A KEY STEP FOR HOW TO FIND AND UNLEASH YOUR ABILITY TO SEE CREATIVELY SO YOU CAN TAKE POWERFUL PHOTOGRAPHS WITH ANY CAMERA

Serena: Moving on to the third step, I would like to ask you what is this third step?

What is the THIRD step beginner photographers need to take with mastering photography techniques and taking beautiful photographs that impress with any camera?

Herbert: Okay. So, I think for this third step, I think would be... I'll try to call it, add a pinch of salt. And by that, what I mean is, if you're cooking, you can cook really good food, but you need a little bit of salt just to give it the finishing flavour.

To give it the *'Wala!'* moment, that delicious flavour in the end. And I think for a lot of people, when you're getting started with a photograph, it feels like cheating that there's an editing process in the end. For most people, they want to take the photograph from the camera and feel like it's complete. And I understand that mindset because that's what I thought in the beginning. I thought, as soon as your photo comes out, it should be done.

And in some cases, it can be completely done, but in most cases it's not. And I'll tell you very quickly why here. So, when I say add a pinch of salt, what I mean is just do a little bit of post-processing or post edit or final retouches to the photo to make the photo really stand out, to really create that message.

The best way to do that is to do very, very simple

tricks like cropping, resizing, colour contrast adjustment etc...

Earlier on, I mentioned that when a person is looking at the photo, the first thing they see is usually the first thing that grabs their attention, is usually where they will start by focusing on.

And so, in the final retouches, it may be that there are still a few more things that are visual and that are standing out and stopping the person from seeing maybe the eyes first, if it was the portrait. And so, what you want to do is you want to make sure you blur them up maybe a little bit more sometimes. Or, sometimes, there is a lot more in the frame of the photograph and you want to crop out, you want to cut them out so that you have the right frame.

And in most cases, you just want to reduce the amount of information inside your work, right? Because if you try to say too much, you overwhelm the person, but if you make the message simple enough, then the message is very, very clear. And so, by adding a pinch of salt, what I mean is, just make your message very, very, very clear to them.

And the way you do that is either remove a few things if there's too much extra or make it so that it's easier to focus where you want them to focus. Or in this case, if there's a color and it's not as bright as you want it to be, just make it a little bit contrasting so that it can be easier to see.

Serena: Oh, okay. So, in this case, it's about being focused on very few elements, which are the most important. In the composition of the picture.

Herbert: Yes.

Serena: One specific example.

Herbert: Okay. So, a specific example of this I'd say is when you're taking portraits. So, when you're taking portraits, usually I think I've used portraits a lot. Let's switch it up. Let's say if you're taking a photo of a house. So, when you're taking a photo of a house, usually what will happen is, the first thing you want to do is you want to set up the house the way you want it. You want to take it from a specific angle, and you want to take it during the right time of the day so that you can see the clouds or blue sky.

So, you have all this setting up and you're done, but the other thing becomes, how do you frame the house? So, most cameras have their own focus settings that you can choose as guide for your frame, but if you noticed a lot of the photographs that you see have many different types of frames. And you also need to realize that some frames look more pleasing than others depending on your photograph.

So, depending on how you want to present that photograph, and we may talk about presentation later, but depending on how you want to present that photograph, you may decide that you need to crop out a few things.

A bit at the bottom where the road is and at the top, and that could be a post-production where you're just cropping out a few things. And then you may decide maybe you want to make the colour of the light inside the house look a little bit brighter, more yellow, so that it looks a more vibrant.

And those could be the few things that you want to do in the post-production process. And I think in this step here, one of the key things I suppose to really, really think about is what you're going to do the photo with. Where the photo is going to be used.

So, the reason why this step is important is... What you want to do is... So, the first step is, you know your message. The second step is, you know your camera and you've taken your photo. The third step is you want to now make sure that your photo is prepared very well, so that where it is placed, the message will speak up. So, for example, if the photo will be displayed in the gallery, it will be on the frame, on the wall.

What colour is the wall? If the wall is white, then you want to pick a frame for the photo that will make the photograph stand out. Or you want to edit the photo in a way that it will stand out if the gallery is white, if the wall is white, because if you make...

Believe it or not, depending on how you process the photo, you may actually make it so that the message is not as impactful.

So, if the photo is being displayed on your website, you want to make sure that the setting that you use in the photo... Sorry, how you're editing the photo will allow the photo to stand out properly on the website. And we may touch a little bit more about this later, but the point here I think is to essentially make it so that there's not too much information. Control the amount of information it's saying so that when the person looks at it, it is as clear as possible. And the best way you do that is by making it simple.

And by making it simple, I just mean reduce or remove some information. Maybe turn it to black and white, or maybe highlight the key colours that you want it to say. It's a creative process. It depends on what you want to achieve, but sometimes just a little bit of extra retouching. If you're doing a portrait, it may be... Some portraits add a lot of setting. Sorry, have a lot of post-production.

There's teeth whitening, eyes whitening. There's nail polishing, there's skin blemishes and removal. There's even hair straightening. There's a lot more that can go into it, but for the basics of this, what I mean is just take a look at the photos and ask yourself, what can you do to improve it? If that makes sense.

Serena: Okay. Thank you for your explanation. And my next question, of course, is about what kind of tools, website types, instruments in general, that our photographers can use to add this pinch of salt?

Herbert: I think in most cases, everyone is going to turn to Photoshop for this and that works. And when I started earlier, there's this small thing called Image... Sorry, I think it's a raw image editor that I used. It's a small element in Photoshop.

Now, I don't know how to use many things. My goal has always been to make my job as simple as possible and what that allowed me to do was to add contrast and control the levels of the colour. And that was all I ever needed. So, for example, if I've taken a photograph, in most cases, it only allowed me to turn it into black and white or to add a small contrast. And I realized just by doing that, you can really create your message because at the end of the day, the goal is to make your message simple.

So, there's going to be a lot of options. Photoshop is one example. Affinity Photo is another example. I've used Affinity Photo. I quite like how their image editor works. And those are the two. I remember one... And it's not important, which one you use, it's more important if you know what you want to achieve, and then you can select the right one because depending on which one you pick...

So, Photoshop will be very good if you want to do some serious, heavy editing where the image raw editor was very good, because when you take a photo in the raw setting format, which means it will come out with a lot of detail. And what you want to do is minimize some of those details by being selective. So, I found that tool to be quite effective in that manner, but there are other tools aside from Affinity. Those are the two most popular ones, and they also have a different pricing. I can't remember what their pricing is, but I know if you buy Affinity, you can buy it once, and then you don't have to keep paying... It's not a subscription model.

So, most people may favour that, but they can do quite about the same in terms of when it comes to photo editing and retouching. And I think Photoshop may also be much, much better for people who may want a lot more editing in cases of portraits or things like that. And you want to edit a lot more. But I've found that both just do about the same. In my case, they all produce the same results in the end.

Serena: So, we can sum up saying that choosing the tool depends on what you want to modify in your picture.

Herbert: Exactly.

Serena: And usually how long does it take for you to modify the picture and the elements that you want to?

Herbert: So, in my case, I would say it depends. It can take between seven to 10 minutes, if it's an event photograph. If it's a portrait, it can take 20 to 30 minutes. And in some cases, if you really, really have to do a very huge portrait, that's going to be maybe printed on a very, very, very big print, then it can take up to an hour.

And the reason because you start to pay attention to the smallest detail possible, but I've never had it take me more than an hour. It's mostly been 20 to 30 minutes per photo. And again, it depends on your message, what you want the photo to say, because sometimes it may mean doing a lot more additional editing.

Serena: I see, I see. Any other suggestions about, let's say, how to get unstuck in case our photographers will have any kind of issues with these tools or with these instruments about modifying and retouching?

Herbert: I think maybe looking at an example, that could be one way, a tutorial example, but in most cases for me, I wouldn't even go to tutorial examples. What I usually do is once I've taken my photographs, I will leave them on my computer, either go for a walk, do something else and then when I come back, I get, I think a small inspiration on how I might process them, because sometimes you want to add that creative element, and so you need to give your mind a space to come up and create and build up that creative element or to have that creative vision.

So, you need to prepare that space in your mind so that you can have that. That's what I found worked for me. So, in most cases that will work, but if you really don't know what setting you're using, then maybe it may be looking at a tutorial and understanding how to achieve what you want to achieve.

If someone was to do this step wrong, what may end up happening is they will get caught up in the editing process and feel like taking photographs is hard because every time they edit, it takes them very, very long. But in reality, it shouldn't. It depends again what you want to do. There are photos where you need to build it up and create something completely new, then the photo becomes too much of an editing process. So, just to be aware of that.

The goal is, you've taken your photo. If you're happy with the message that it's saying, then the only thing you want to do here is just make it so that the message is very clear because people, when they're looking at the photograph, they're scrolling down or they're looking on their website, they don't have much time.

They only have about three seconds to decide, and that's a very small amount of time. So, the easier it is to see your message in the photo, the better it is for the person who is looking to say, "ah, so that's what it's saying."

Serena: Okay. So, the main message is, if you get stuck, take a small break, empty your mind, be focused on something else to be ready.

Herbert: Yes.

Serena: That makes sense.

THE NEXT STEPS FOR BEGINNER PHOTOGRAPHERS

Serena: Are there any other beginner steps at this point with mastering photography techniques, we need to let our photographers know about when getting started?

Herbert: Yeah, I can think of one and that is how you present your work. So, present your work. And this is actually, I've seen even professional photographers, I've seen them not do it, and it's a small step that makes all the difference...

I think I briefly mentioned earlier, know where your photograph will be presented. If your photograph is going to be on a magazine, then you want to understand what colour is the magazine, because it makes all the difference.

I have made this mistake myself, where the photo looks so much well on a computer, but on the print, the colours were completely different. So, understanding that and being prepared for that. Having the right settings for that.

And then the other thing is presenting. There's presentation so that the photo looks right, but there's also presentation so that the message is right. So, for example, I mentioned if the wall's white, making sure you pick colours that will help your photo stand out, or maybe that will highlight, or maybe that will create a frame around your photo. So, thinking about things like that. How you present your work is really key to making sure that your message comes across.

And when the person looks at it, they get your message right away. And the best way to really master this step very, very quickly is...

I think will be to learn by example. I can't think of any shortcuts. It's really to learn by example, to find examples. And in most cases, the photos will not be printed, but if you're going to upload your photos to platforms like Instagram and Pinterest, understand that there's different formats that work best for those platforms. If you're going to upload it to a website, understand what way you can make your photographs look best.

And if you're going to give your photograph to a client, understand that your client does not know a thing about photography. And you gave them a photo with very large data like raw formats. They are still going to use it on their website, even though that will be harmful.

It will slow down their website and everything. So, you want to be that good photographer who maybe makes the job easier for your clients, for yourself, and make your work stand out. So, there are things that you can do to prepare. So, knowing what you can do, depending on what you want to show, where you want to show your work, can

	make a huge difference. I think that would be the one additional thing that I can think of.
Serena:	Okay. So, the main focus is about how to present your work.
Herbert:	Exactly.
Serena:	The first step is about learning from example. And then I would say experience and expertise will do the rest.
Herbert:	Yes.

MASTERING PHOTOGRAPHY TECHNIQUES TOOLS EVERY PHOTOGRAPHER NEEDS

Serena: Speaking again about tools.

Are there any tools for mastering photography techniques our photographers need to know about here as it's start of their journey? So, something that they should know from the very beginning.

Herbert: I think I would say, take the camera and shoot. One of the things I've heard, and I've seen it over and over again in the photography community, they say the best camera is the camera you have. And I think that touches back with what I was saying, which was know your camera, right?

I'd say, know what your camera can do to help you create what you want to create. So, I don't think you'd need more tools but rather knowing how to create that with what you have.

You don't need to buy the latest phone to take good photography, and you don't need to buy the latest camera, lens and gear to take the best camera photograph. All you need to do is essentially just know what message you want to create, manipulate the environment, know what your camera can do or what it's limits are, and then try to work within those limits.

And then with a little bit of post editing, adding the final retouches, that's it. You should be able to create about any message with any camera.

Serena: So, mostly it's about what we've been talking about until now. Clients, camera, your motivation, settings and experimenting in that setting.

Herbert: Yes.

THE PERFECT MINDSET FOR PHOTOGRAPHERS

Serena: We will now talk about one of, let's say, the keywords, and we talk about mindset. I have a question for you about this.

What is the perfect mindset for a beginner photographer at this point that would virtually guarantee their success?

Or put it another other words…

What is the right mindset for photographers when it comes to getting started taking beautiful photographs that impress with any camera?

Herbert: Okay. So, I think the best way I can say is I think there's different ways to think of a creative art process, and depending on the individual, but what I have found is there are three ways to think about this mindset.

One is the type of creative process is the creative process where you are adding information. So, if you look at drawings and paintings, the artist has to add every stroke of brush and stroke of pencil to build up the artwork to the end. And that will be adding material or information to build up the piece of art.

And then the other process will be the process where you're taking away material or information. And in this case, it will be a sculpture who starts with a very big chunk of rock or marble. And then starts chipping away the bits of marble to the point where they have a very beautiful statue, right?

And another creative process will be the creative process where you are moulding, you're shaping what you already have.

And this would be the example of a person blowing glass and moulding it into shape and then to create a piece of artwork. And so, there's all this, which I think they are the three creative processes. And if you're going to take photography, I think photography can actually fit in any of those three, depending on how you use it. And I'll give you a very brief example here.

There are photographs where you can take one photo and then you can add so much information to transform it in the post edition process, to transform it into something completely new that says the message you want. So graphic design would be one example… so if you ever look at movie posters that how that was created…

So, that means you're building up with a lot of different photos, adding different elements in the editing process to create what you want. And then in other cases, it's just about editing what you have, to get the most of what you have, which will be using just the moulding process, or you can use the process of removing as much information to create the message that you want. A good example of this is if you look at music posters… like Celine Dion's music Album cover or similar musicians…

And I think as a photographer, sometimes you need to be thinking which of these processes you're going to be used before you take a photo, or when you're taking a photo. And the reason is because if you're looking at an event or if you're just looking at a scenery and you want to take a photo of it, unless you can think of a process, sometimes it's going to be a little bit tricky to figure out how can I show my message, but if you're aware of this processes, then you can think, okay, if I remove that and that and that, I can create this.

Or you can think, okay, this looks good, but if I add all these things together, I can create this message. So, it's about thinking of those processes. And that's what really, really helps you build the artwork which you want.

And I think that is one of the key, best mindsets that has really, really helped me a lot, because what you will notice is two people can take the same photograph, but they can present very, very differently as well, just depending on what they're focusing on and what elements they are using.

And another mindset to use will be something that we touched earlier on… Asking

"what does my client want to achieve, and how can I help them achieve that?"

And with that mindset, when you combine with

this, then it becomes clear as in what you can do to reach your end goal. So, these are really to help you create more without getting stuck as a creator. If that makes sense.

Serena: Okay. So, let's say the right mindset is composed from a clear purpose. You have your picture, the goal of your client and a creative process.

Herbert: Yeah. In a way it is, because at the end of the day, what you want to do is you want to be able to create without getting stuck. And so, you need to think, what can I do here to achieve the results that I want?

Serena: You have been very clear, but still I'm wondering if there is anything that I haven't asked you about getting started with mastering photography techniques that you'd like to share with our audience of photographers.

Herbert: I think I've shared everything in terms of mindset and being prepared. And I think if the photographer can master those previous steps, they can really achieve their desired the end result very fast.

Serena: Okay.

MASTERING PHOTOGRAPHY TECHNIQUES TIME WASTERS

Serena: Now, I would like to talk and ask about the topic of the time, if you agree. My first question is about waste of time, and to be more specific, I would like to ask you…

Where do you see beginner photographers wasting a lot of time in mastering photography techniques?

Herbert: Okay. In most cases, most photographers, the biggest challenge they face is when you are starting; usually there's a lot of things with photography. With photography, one of the best ways to explain it is, it's a skill that requires mastering a tool that is capable of so much more, but you only need to master one particular element to create your message, right?

For example, you only need to master the settings for portraits to take a very good portrait, an artistic portrait. And so the biggest part where most photographers really, really get stuck in is getting the right knowledge in. The way they will get stuck in this situation will be, they will be trying to get a lot of camera equipment. They'll buy studio lights. They'll try to get a camera flash. They'll try to get studio lights. They'll try to get a portrait lens, zoom lens, telephoto lens, and micro lens.

They'll try to get just about every single tool, including filters. I myself am guilty because at the beginning I was watching this tutorial, and this guy convinced me perfectly well that I needed filters. So I went and bought filters for every one of my lens, and they were expensive.

They're like 50 euros per filter, that's an equivalent of around $55 per filter. And if you're buying it for three, four lenses, you've just already spent at least over $200 over something that you don't really need because you don't really need filters for your cameras, unless you're trying to achieve a specific effect. But in this case, the filters I got were not even filters to achieve an effect, they were just more to keep the lens clean.

And then I realized, actually, you do not need that. All you need is a piece of clothing, a very such clothing that is used for wiping glasses, eyeglasses. You can use that to wipe your lens if there's anything, but in most cases, you'll learn to survive perfectly. Ever since I've removed the filters years ago, I haven't needed even to clean my lens at the front. They are always clean because I always covered them as soon as I finished using them. So a lot of photographers will get lost on this journey where you end up buying so many things that you do not need.

And as a way to know, if you're going down this rabbit hole, one of these guys that I used to interact with when we were taking photographs, trying to exchange tips and ideas, he said, "the only time you should really considering you should go and buy something is when you're thinking you've taken all the photo's... If you've taken all the photos really, really well, and you're still feeling, if only I had this, then you feel like it's the time maybe to upgrade."

But in most cases, you don't because you still have a lot more to master within the equipment. So, where they're wasting time, it's wasting time on buying things and wasting time on learning the wrong skills, because there's so much to learn and there's so many things you could learn. And that is why I suggested starting with understanding why do you want to take that photo?

Because by understanding your message, then you only focus on what you need to help you achieve your goal.

MASTERING PHOTOGRAPHY TECHNIQUE AND TIME MANAGEMENT

Serena: So, perfect. And, speaking about time, if you explain to us, with some advices or tips, what is the best way possible they could manage it.

Herbert: So any tips for time management when it comes to mastering photography, yeah?

Serena: Exactly.

Herbert: Okay. One of the biggest things that you wouldn't know as a photographer until you become a photographer, and it's like an inside thing, is that photography actually takes quite a lot of time than you would realize. And in this case, if you take a case of where you're taking photographs for a client, one thing you realize is you need to prepare the day before.

And the day before what you want to do is you want to make sure your cameras are charged. If you're using two cameras, or if you're just using one camera, you want to make sure you have a spare battery for that camera in case you go over time, and you want to make sure that everything is in order, your lens, your camera settings are in order.

So that when you go during the day, even if you are, let's say, a minute late because of who God knows what happened, traffic in the morning or things happen, right? We live in the real world, so things happen. You want to make sure you've prepared your gear, so when you get there, you can just pull out your camera and start shooting. This also goes for when you're traveling.

You want to make sure that you've prepared your gear, so when you get there, you just put on your lens and you start shooting and getting those photos, getting those action shots very, very quickly without having to try and set it up. And also when you're preparing for the night before, usually what you want to make sure is you've packed everything you need from your camera, your flash batteries are charged. Your camera flash batteries if you're using that.

But if you're not using that, the other thing that you want to make sure you're prepared is, you want to know the venue and you want to know the people that you're going to be photographing. In most cases, it may be worth maybe looking into who you'll be taking photographs of because just knowing makes a lot of difference because you could be taking photos of someone really, really important. And if you do not know that, you may be focusing on the wrong people.

This is something that happens when you're taking photographs of very important keynote speakers, or maybe very important photographs of meetings that are documenting a very important occasion taking place, and so this may be the case.

In some cases, the client, you can ask them "who will I be photographing, what or who should I be focusing on?" and they will tell you. They'll tell you, but most clients will not know this because they expect the photographer is an expert. And so you want to get there and be ready. You want to be their expert. And so doing your homework beforehand.

The other thing that you want to make sure you...

You need to pay attention to...so, you prepared your camera the night before, you've gotten there, you're ready, you've taken the photographs of everything important, you haven't missed a moment. Then you have a post-production process, and this is also where it's going to take you a lot of time.

Now, if you have been following the process from the beginning that I mentioned, as in you know why you're taking photographs and everything, that means in each and every shot, in each and every shoot, you will have confidence knowing that you have taken the photo you want, a photo that tells the story, a photo that is emotional, a photo that is very, very impactful.

Even if you're documenting your family's life, you have taken a photo that you know really captured the moment and represented what you wanted it to present, because you knew what you were looking for, right? You had your reasons why you've taken that photo, so because you know this, what it means is when you're taking the photograph, you already know how many photos you think you got before you even open them up.

When you load them to the computer, you start sorting out your photo. And this is where a lot of time will be wasted. This actually can take up to an hour to two hours to sort them out if not done correctly, and so this is where you want to also be sure that you have a process for sorting out, selecting the ones you want, and quickly processing them.

And processing them could mean just highlighting key elements, cropping out the photographs, making sure they're framed properly. And also making sure that each of the photographs that you took essentially is represented in a way that the client can use. For example, if they want them for a website, if they want them for print, they want them for...

So, there's a website, for print, for brochure, there's also for banner, which is a much, much bigger version of a print. And so you want to make sure that you have the right formats for those. And so what I do is usually I have a system for saving photographs, but you also make sure you've asked your client to tell you all this information, what do they want the photos for?

So, when you're processing, you know, so that it saves you time because you do not want to be going back and forward with your client too many times.

And if you're taking photos for a hobby, this is just when you select your three to four or five good photos, and then you process them. And then the rest you want to save them somewhere else where they will not take up your computer's storage space.

And another thing that I had forgotten to mention a little bit is, is that by trying to manage your time, you'll find yourself that a lot of the work you do, photography will only take about 25%, and the rest will really be about managing and keeping everything within balance.

And the best way to do that is to start early and to start creating, to create to document what you're doing, and then follow it as a process, improving on it each and every single time.

There is no one size fits all because many, many photographers use many, many different processes, but by documenting what you're doing, you can always improve on it. And I found that to be the best way possible.

Serena: Thank you very much for your precious tips, and I hope our photographers have really taken notes of all of these suggestions.

THE TOP MASTERING PHOTOGRAPHY TECHNIQUES CHALLENGES BEGINNER PHOTOGRAPHERS FACE

Serena: Now, I would like to change the topic a bit and talk about the challenges.

What are the big challenges for beginners in mastering photography techniques right now?

Herbert: Okay. One of the things that I've learned and I've seen is that the challenges really come down to, I think, understanding what you're doing, because like I said, it's a skill that you could get lost in knowing the camera. You could always use the auto mode and get everything you want, but the challenges come when you try to do too much and not realize you're actually trying to do too much, or trying to do too little and not realizing that you've been limiting your creative ability.

And that's why I strongly believe starting with why is the best. Before you pick up your camera, if you ask yourself why, what message do I want to say? Because at the end of the day, it's going to take your time and effort, and it can be a challenge to do something if you're not really sure exactly.

And another biggest challenge that photographers will face is confidence. And what do I mean by that? To go from a beginner photographer to a pro photographer, it takes confidence. It takes confidence in your work. It takes a lot of pressure. It takes a lot of, what do you call this, mental... There's a lot of self- belief that goes into there, because you've created this piece.

In most cases you may not have had the chance to get a good reaction that you wanted, and the reason why you didn't get that good reaction is, for whatever reason, maybe you haven't shown enough people to get a good reaction. I was lucky enough a lot of my friends were very supportive.

They convinced me to try photography, as in, to push my photography, because they had seen work that wasn't substandard. And so they believed the quality and the standard was already there in my work, and they didn't see why I didn't do it.

It took a lot of people selling me the point I should try. But one of the key things that I've learned, that is absolutely crucial to overcoming the idea of these confidence of the challenge is very, very simple. If you want to master it in 30 days, the process that I would use is first to begin all over again. This is what I will do. The first week I'll take my camera.

I'll pick whatever type of photography I want to practice, whether it's animal photography, portrait photography, event photography, travel photography, family photography, real estate photography, landscape, whichever one, I'll just pick one of those.

And for the first week, I'll practice just shooting

with the one setting and making sure that I'm getting the photo to tell my message for the first week. And then for the second week, I'll start showing my friends who I know have an interest in this area, in this photograph. And I'll start showing them, taking photos.

The idea here is I'm starting showing them these photos on my website. First week I'm taking them, putting them on my website. Second week I'm showing them. It doesn't matter how good they are, how good my website is, I'm just focusing on showing them. And from there, I'll get the reaction and feedback. And from there, I'll get words that will help me tell my message.

For example, if they've seen the location, they may say things like, "wow, that looks exactly like when I was there," or they may say things like,

"wow, she looks exactly like her. Wow, how did he get her? What was she looking at?"

Those kinds of reactions mean that you're doing the right thing. And so by getting those kinds of reactions, you're also getting people to look at your work, but you are getting people to talk about your work.

If you are focusing about clients, this is also where people who have seen your work may start recommending you to their friends who are trying to get photos. And this is where you start getting your first clients. Ideally with your first clients, what you do is you are really working out the price, for example. And when you're getting started, pricing of your work could be very, very tricky. One thing is, you have no confidence.

Two is, you have never done it. And so how you would... When I started, how I priced it was, I just went for the lowest price I could think of. And I went for the cost of how much it'll cost me to work, so my travel costs, my, maybe, gear repair costs and things like that, and then I went with that. And what I realized you can also do is, you can also go with, I need to buy this thing, and I think if you can help me get that, I can take for you those photos.

It becomes a way for trade because they want photos from you. So, here, what I'm saying is, the first week you practice. The second week you are getting people to see your work while you're still practicing and adding. And within that, you may also start getting clients. And then from there on the goal is just then build the relationship and keep really improving.

The improvements will only keep coming as you go. But the idea is you pick one area. You are focused. Notice that I haven't mentioned that you should go to the shop and start buying the equipment before you try. But what I'm saying is, once you've already focused, you're already showing people, then you start to see things that you may need to help you show your work even better. And what that means is that some of your work may even pay for itself.

One of the things that I was very lucky about, I used this strategy myself and my first camera that I got in Canada paid for all the equipment. I even managed to buy a photography studio, a small photography studio. And it was my first camera, the basic camera that helped me pay for all of those.

So yeah, I think that's the best way to go about this challenge, which is the confidence, is to really take photos, share with people, and allow them to tell you what they think, how they see it, so you can learn from how other people see your work.

Serena: Good. Okay, so that was very, very interesting. Mainly we are starting it from getting confidence then step-by-step to get feedback, and from that step on to learn more and more about how to sell, let's say, your work.

HIDDEN MASTERING PHOTOGRAPHY TECHNIQUES OPPORTUNITIES

Serena: I understood very well. From big challenges, let's step to big opportunities.

Where are the big opportunities in mastering photography techniques that many beginners or even experienced photographers might be missing, in your opinion?

Herbert: That's a good question, actually. And I like that question because I think opportunities and challenges and go together hand in hand. Where there's a challenge, there's always an opportunity. I'm a big believer of that. For example, my favourite type of photography is really people.

I like photographing people. I can never get enough of the expressions that a human can communicate by just the simple gestures that they do, and I think capturing that is forever fascinating.

No matter how many times they've been painted, there's always opportunity. And the other thing I'm a big believer of is that, for example, when you're studying, you're asking yourself, why am I doing this? Why am I taking this photograph? And by asking that question, why, a beginning, then the question becomes, well, where are the opportunities within what I want to do?

For example, one of the reasons why I take photographs is I wanted to help my clients, I still do, to help my clients really show how impactful, emotional, captivating, and empowering the events were. I wanted to help the person show how powerful, basically to show who they really are. The best way I can show them is how unique they are because we are all very different and unique, and we all have our own moments that make us look like we're shining. And to be able to show that in the photograph, I thought, was a very powerful thing.

So I think the challenges are, if you decide, let's say, to take animal photographs, then the goal is to really truly ask yourself... Sorry, I think the opportunity... If you decide to take photographs of animals, then opportunity comes when you decide to ask yourself, well, if I want to photograph animals, who are the people who want the animals photograph? Maybe the people who are selling pets, or maybe selling pet food, or maybe the zoos.

And so, by looking at there, you begin to see a lot of opportunities, but these opportunities do not diminish. They expand, depending on how you use your network effect. So earlier on, I said, taking your photographs and showing your friends, and then from there start getting clients.

But what I didn't mention is, this thing, and which I think is a very big opportunity, when you're taking the photos for your clients, it's not the same as taking a photo for yourself. When you're taking a photo for your clients, if you are thinking about how can I help my client achieve this better, and if you do that, they will see it. Nine times out of 10, they will see it, and when they do see that they will appreciate that. And they will come back to you for that. They will come back to you, and they will ask you for more work.

They will talk about your work. They will promote your work. And this is how you get a client from a one time customer to become a repeat client. A lot of my clients are repeat. As a matter of fact, I never ran any ads. They were always just coming back to me, recommending me to other people to the point where I was like,

"Oh my God, that's a lot of people coming. I can't handle all this. I'm just one person."

And this all happens because you are doing your work right. And so that's where the opportunity is coming in, doing your work right. By doing your work right, I don't mean you need to invent a new photography technique. God no, I don't mean that. What I mean is very simple. If you're going to take photographs for your client to use on their website, then make the photos so that when they are using them on their website, they will be very high quality to look at, but they won't slow their website down.

And the way you do that is just by saving them with the right setting. If your client's website is a black background, then make sure that the photographs will match with whatever colours it is, so that when someone looks it stands out. If your client's website is pink or blue, then you make sure that the photographs will match because at the end of the day, you are producing work for your client. They don't know anything.

They just believe you're an expert. So, by being the expert and all, it has to do is just being considerate, and just go that small extra mile when you present your work. Usually what I do is I present my work in two folders, two separate folders of photographs. I would say, these are photographs for website, these are for social media, or these are for websites and these are for print.

Usually I would have asked my clients, so I know these things. And by doing that, you create yourself opportunities, because if I am a client and I'm getting these photos which are ready for website, I can just plug them in. But if I'm getting these photographs and I have no idea, I can use them, but the problem that comes with using those photographs may stop me from coming back because...

You do not want to create problems for them, make it easier for them to give you more opportunities. If it's about work, getting more work, then also picking the right, maybe, photography type.

For example, event photography, there's always events throughout the year, so that'll be one way to see it as an event opportunity. There's always events coming up. Wedding photography, there's always weddings coming up. I think there's a lot of endless ways to capture photography, but it's about how you approach the subject to maximize opportunities. I hope that answered the question.

Serena: It did. There are plenty of examples useful to understand how to change and how to transform challenges in opportunities. The main point is, be focused on your client, his or her needs, and his or her desires.

Herbert: Absolutely. Absolutely.

A MASTERING PHOTOGRAPHY TECHNIQUES CASE STUDY

Serena: You've been very, very clear till this moment. Next question is one of my favourites, because it's about experience.

Is there one particular story, case study or example you'd like to share that really sums up what we've been talking about here?

Herbert: Okay. So a case study of, I suppose, everything that I've been talking about up until now, correct?

Serena: Yes.

Herbert: Okay. I think the best example of all this is when I first got started. In the very early days, I was hired by a client to take photographs, to take photographs of portraits. It was a very last minute call to go and take photographs the next day. I did what I always did, prepare everything the night before, and then when I got to the shoot, my camera was ready and everything. I knew my environment. I knew the location that we'll be photographing. And so we started taking photographs of them.

I had to take photographs of about 15, I think, 10 to 15 clients within an hour, so I had really about five minutes each. If remember correctly I had five minutes with each, so I don't know how many we had to push, and then the rest we photographed after.

These were clients that were busy with during their working hours, and so it was really getting them as fast as possible. And then, within those five minutes, I was supposed to prepare everything I needed to take photographs, get to know the client.

Get to know the subject, and then take the photograph, professional photographs for their website, and then so on. One thing I noticed was... I took all the photos, no sweat and everything, and I knew I had all the photographs that... I knew I had at least one photograph that each client liked. But in most cases, I always make sure I have at least four or five, four to five that they really like, so they have an option.

Giving people options, I've learned, is a really good way to make some feel assured, but not too many options that they get a mental block. So I had options. And in this case I had photographs. One of the participants was David. I had taken a photo of him, and on this particular occasion, his photos were my favourite photos I had ever taken up until then, and I think up until today actually and just because I had really managed to allow him to express himself. You may or may not know this, but when you're trying to get a subject or participant to express himself during a photography session, it can be quite difficult. And the reason is because either people are just uncomfortable with the camera, it's a weird thing trying looking at you to capture a moment.

And some people, maybe, not so uncomfortable, but it's just that for some people, it's hard to relax. You're always meant to be representable, and especially if you're a guy and trying to get another guy, another man to express themselves in a way that shows them their very best form, it can be challenging.

And so, it's easier to have a way of controlling that environment as a photographer, so that when you take a photograph, they come out as natural as possible. And so in this particular case, I had managed to really do that very well, and so all the participants were really very well clear.

I was proud to have taken these photos, and I was really excited to show David the next time we meet and explain. But unfortunately, just about the week after I had taken, after processing, I got a call. The call was that there had been an unfortunate event, and David had passed away during his holidays up in the US in a car accident. I got the call and it didn't make too much of...

I didn't know how to process it at the time, and it took me awhile. But what they were asking was for me to create another set of photos where they'll be presenting them for their family, because they couldn't find any more recent photos.

So my photo was basically the last photo that they

could come up and use. And so I prepared a few photos, and then I selected. The moment hit me when all of David co-workers we were looking at the photos, and they kept saying words like, "wow, that's so much like him and he was like that."

And not only did that hit me, but I also realized something in that moment there that I had come to understand him and feel connected. I didn't understand it at the time, but I attempt to feel connected more than...

Maybe, to really connect to another human being at a level that I had never understood before because my goal had always been to understand the fears, roadblocks, desires, and maybe even their goals, so that I can help them reach their goals, show them how confident they are, how approachable they are, so I can help them reach their goals.

But in the process of doing that, I had gotten to know them in a five-minute period in a humane and meaningful way than I understood. I had gotten to know them so much better than I had realized. So when this happened, it was quite a shock, but it also taught me a very big lesson.

And that is, we are doing this work for another human being, whether it's showing them a message so that they can take the right action, or it's showing them a message that they can save a life, or whether it's just preserving a memory. In this case, I found my photo to be used for quite a very different reason than I had set out for it to be used. And so, I suppose that captures the whole idea that you're photographing for other humans. Only humans even interact with this photograph, and maybe other beings too, but it's going to be mostly humans.

They're going to look at these, and so maybe photographing with that perspective in mind. So that kind of sums up the idea of, maybe, everything that I was talking about as in how to approach something so that it speaks to other fellow humans, and it's not just work, but it's more than work.

Serena: Thanks for sharing this touching, peculiar, and unusual episode. In my opinion, it represents the way how photography links people's lives and changes them forever in a way, in your case and in his family's case as well. And yes, I truly agree with what I heard from you. Photo is not only about taking pictures, you're not just doing this click on your camera, but it's about getting in touch with people. You will understand and you will found out more about the person who is on the opposite side of the lens.

Herbert: Yes.

Serena: That's very, very important, and I hope that our listeners understood this aspect of their job. We are close to the end of the interview.

FINAL THOUGHTS FROM MASTERING PHOTOGRAPHY TECHNIQUES EXPERT HERBERT INNOCENT

Serena: So, one of the questions that I would like to ask you is about, what final thoughts do you have to help motivate the beginner photographers to get started with mastering their photographic technique?

Herbert: Okay.

In terms of final thoughts, I think the one thought I can really, really think of is to really grab the camera and then go and take photographs. Take a photo and don't even worry about it too much. And the reason being is, I have photographed a lot with my friend. We would go and take evening photographs, morning, day, as I mentioned earlier, we've taken a lot of photographs. And one of the things I have learned is, we went to the same places, but we took so many different photos. Her photos were so much different from mine.

I was surprised at every single turn. It didn't matter how many times we did it, it surprised me. It's almost as if we were paying to the different parts, we were paying attention to the different parts of this world. And so that says a lot about how unique we really are. We are individuals with individual perspectives.

And so, take a photograph even if it's about your family, because it may be the one chance you get to show them a small part of your world that they may otherwise never get to see. And if you're really that much into it, then just master the first three steps, really. And then you should be able to really help them get closer, help them get closer to each other, to you, or to whoever you want them to get closer to because it is another language that we have that allows us to speak, maybe not through words, but through whatever visual means, which is...

What we see is what we believe. It's what we follow, it's what... We do a lot of things because of what we can see. And so I think the final thought will be, you are unique, so show the world how unique, your unique world, what you see. Show people your point of view of this world. Your voice matters. Your voice matters, and what you see matters a lot.

Serena: Oh, that's very poetic, and I like how you underline the human aspect, I would like to say, of your job or of a photographer's job. So, ending, I would define this a privilege to get closer to someone that basically is a stranger for you, but you give to them, and they gave to you in a way; it's from both sides, the chance to show people their unique personality, let's say, and to show them your voice and the messages that they want to say to the rest of the world, I think.

Herbert: Absolutely.

WHERE TO FROM HERE...

Serena: Before we will close, I would like to ask you, on behalf of our listeners, our audience, how can people find out more about you, about your job, about your pieces of art?

Herbert: Innocent Photography, that'd be one place, and yeah.

Serena: This is your website?

Herbert: Yes, that's my website, InnocentPhotography.com

I also have a resource web-page there to help beginner photographers and clients…

Serena: Let's re-recommend our audience to go and navigate, to find out some of your best work.

Herbert: Yes.

Serena: We are at the end of our interview.

I want to thank you Herbert Innocent for this great interview.

I'm sure all the photographers in our audience have a much clearer understanding of getting started with mastering photography technique now that you have laid everything out so clearly.

So, thank you very much for sharing your expertise and experiences so graciously.

Well done, and thank you all the photographers in our audience for joining us for this amazing beginners guide presentation.

Have a great day.

Herbert: Thank you.

MEET HERBERT INNOCENT

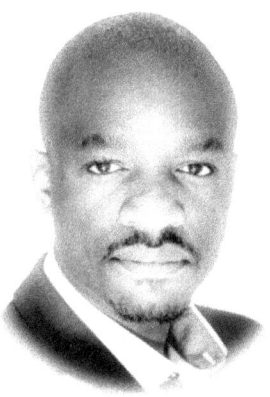

Herbert Innocent is an expert in mastering photography techniques whose accomplishments include:

Education:

- Studied Bio-Medical Engineering at The University of Trinity College Dublin
- Self-taught Corporate Photographer

Work History:

- Taken over 10 000+ paid for photographs of some of the most special moments, from inspiring corporate event photography all the way to wedding photography...
- 4+ years in Corporate photography Shooting, editing and professional retouching

- Built a photography business while in college and landed some of the big business clients while I was still a student
- Got a ton of new clients and repeat clients without ever spending a dollar on Ads

Awards, Titles, and Designations:

- Photographs have been features in leading Newspapers, Brochures, Clients websites, Books and Booklets
- Won a photography competition with my best friend in Junior high for being a good kid
- Has been published before

Personal Info:

- Went from zero to a professional corporate photographer in a few short months while teaching myself photography techniques
- Got my first camera after working in a Summer Camp up in the mountains of Canada…
- Used that first basic camera to pay for all the new photography gears and even bought a little photography studio using the very principles in this book.
- Was diagnosed with Tuberculosis at 23…

Most of what you need is instruction and encouragement from someone who has "been there and done that!" with how to find and unleash your ability to see creatively so you can take powerful photographs with any camera.

And as you can see, mastering photography techniques expert Herbert Innocent is uniquely qualified to help you understand everything you need to know about taking beautiful photographs that impress with any camera!

If you would like to learn more visit

www.behindthecameralens.com

or you can email us at

info@behindthecameralens.com

All the best with Mastering your Photography Techniques

www.ingramcontent.com/pod-product-compliance
Lightning Source LLC
Chambersburg PA
CBHW071414210526
45465CB00001B/390